Frozen Fences
Brady Kent & John Ashton

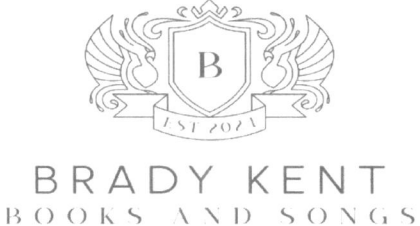

Copyright

2024 Frozen Fences by Brady Kent & John Ashton
Poems: Brady Kent: © copyright of Brady Kent
Images: John Ashton: © copyright of John Ashton
All rights reserved. Published by Brady Kent Books.

Brady Kent has asserted his right to be identified as the author of this work in accordance with the copyright, designs and patents act 1998.

No part of this book can be reproduced or stored in any form, written, electronic or mechanical, including photography, recording, or by any information retrieval system without written permission by the author. Although every precaution has been taken in the preparation of this book, the publisher/author assume no responsibility for errors or omissions.

Neither is any liability assumed for damages resulting from the use of information contained herein.

Website: www.brand.page/bradykentpoet
E Mail: www.bradykentpoet@gmail.com
Soundcloud: www.soundcloud.com/discover
LinkedIn: www.linkedin.com/in/brady-kent
TikTok: www.tiktok.com/@bradykent
Facebook:www.facebook.com/BradyKentPoet
X: www.Brady Kent (@BradykentPoet) / X
Instagram: www.instagram.com/bradykentpoet
YouTube: www.youtube.com/@Bradykent-d5w

Preface

These poems and images are a collaboration between longtime friends, Brady Kent and John Ashton.

Our aim was to examine the details contained within landscapes, through words and photographs.

While some show scenes of abandonment or decay, each retains a beauty and significance, perhaps inspiring a deeper layer of understanding.

Brady Kent and John Ashton

Also by Brady Kent

Politics and Poems
Sentiments and Poems
Story Telling Song Lyrics
Fire Escape
Improvised Song Lyrics
Frozen Fences
Rhythm and Blues Song Lyrics
Emotions and Song Lyrics

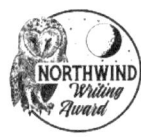

Contents

Gate	6
Precarious	8
Light through trees	10
Road, man, dog	12
Face on a stone (Castlerigg)	14
Internet killed the video store	16
Allium seedhead	18
Frozen fence	20
Loneliest bus stop	22
The hidden lake	24
Light in the cloud	26
The signpost	28
Daybreak	30

Frozen Fences
Brady Kent & John Ashton

Gate

Guarding. Guarding what is not
clear.

Who lived there? Who lives there
now?

The gate remains unopened,
no soul ever steps through.

A gate without purpose.

Like stinging nettles, wasps or
ulcers, or ageing executives
fired, paid off.

No road to guide our way
in or out.

Not even a muddy trail.

Dark clouds scour in anger,
unable to rain on strangers.

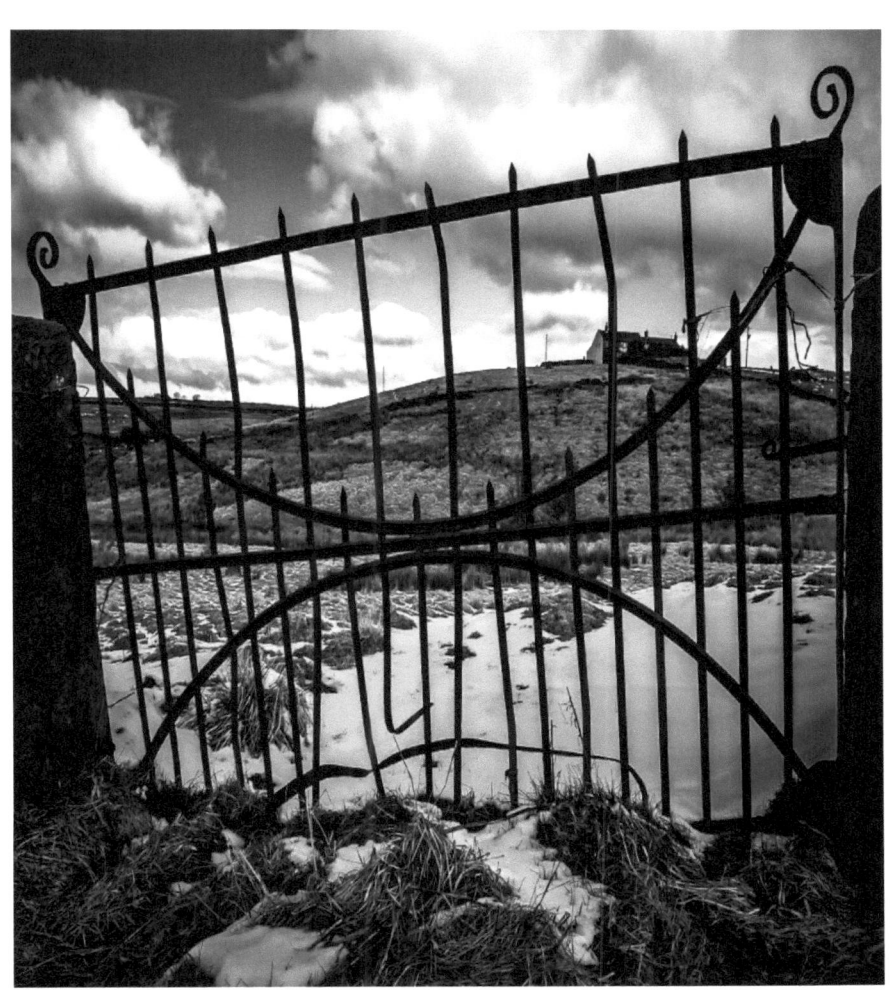

Precarious

Built and rebuilt so many times, this former wall has become a joke.

Right rocks in wrong places. Usurped by wire, barbed and otherwise.

No longer a singular edifice, its disparate pieces perfectly aligned.

Not soldiers on parade. More like mercenaries, guerrillas in war's confusion.

And yet it survives the years, maybe decades.

Shouting, 'Look at me! I'm a tower! See how I balance!"

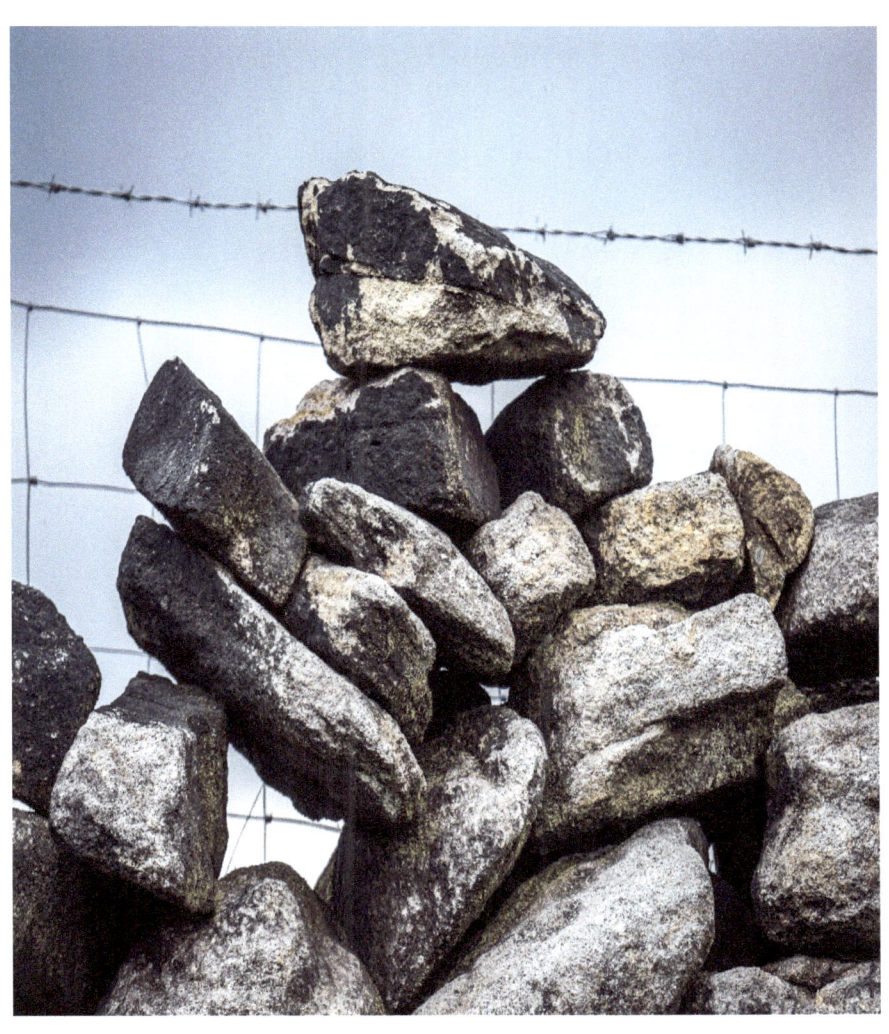

Light through trees

An unkempt yet unmistakable gateway.

A green passage, formed by a gap in the trees. The light will guide us through.

Manicured bushes beyond, offer the hope, even promise of order, symmetry, stability.

A better future.

There are tracks, barely visible. As if meaning to be unseen. Or seen and used by someone unknown to us.

Still the opening seduces. Physical, natural, it charms but is mysterious.

Where does it lead? Shall we go through and risk all?

Does heaven have a foyer, when called?

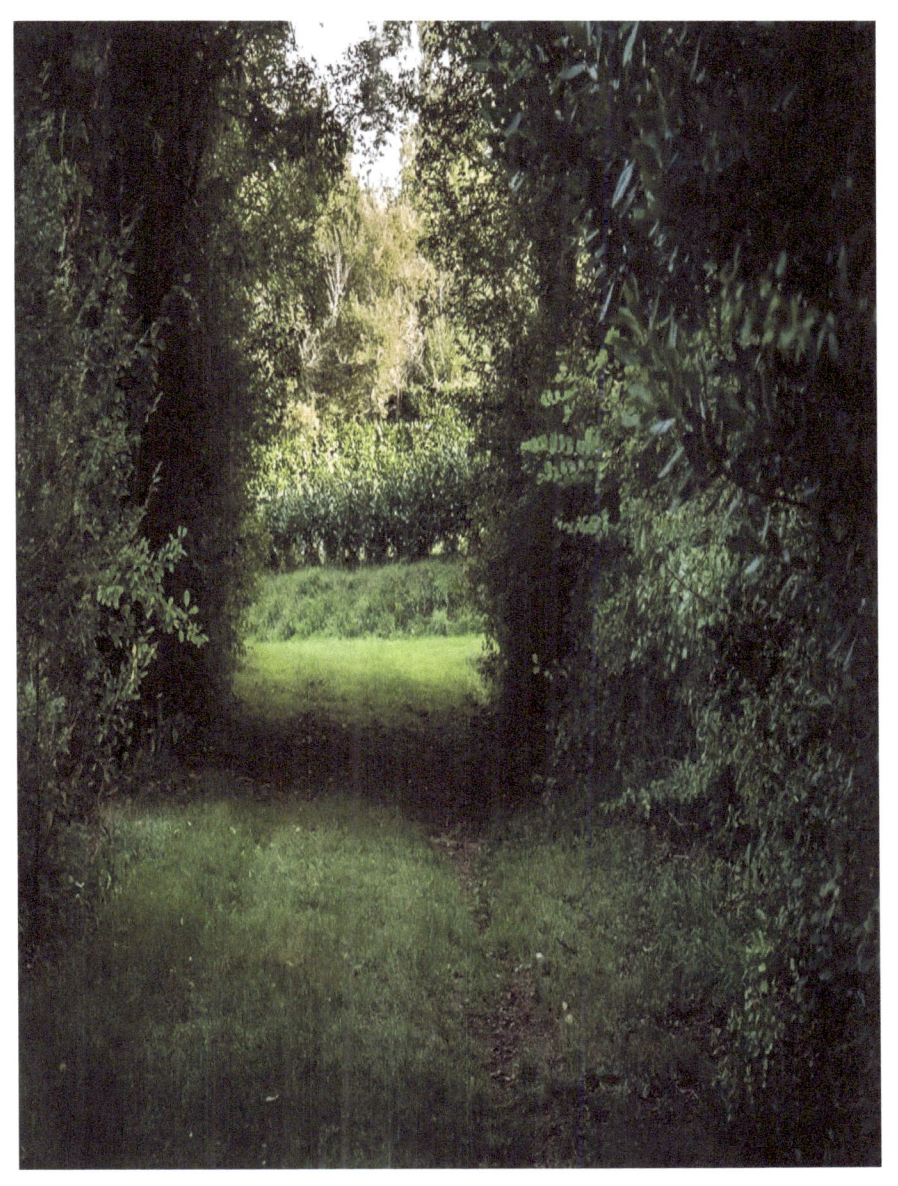

Road, man, dog

Four hills, a man, a dog and a pole,
twelve sheep like watching apostles.

Too far to any destination, too far to
turn and trudge back.

A road from a fairy forest of furs, a
place where creatures live and die.

A loyal dog that leads the way, to help
his master to discover the way home.

The heather does not care who patrols,
who survives, who achieves their goals.

With no stiles in sight, there is no short
cut, or way of troubling the dozen sheep.

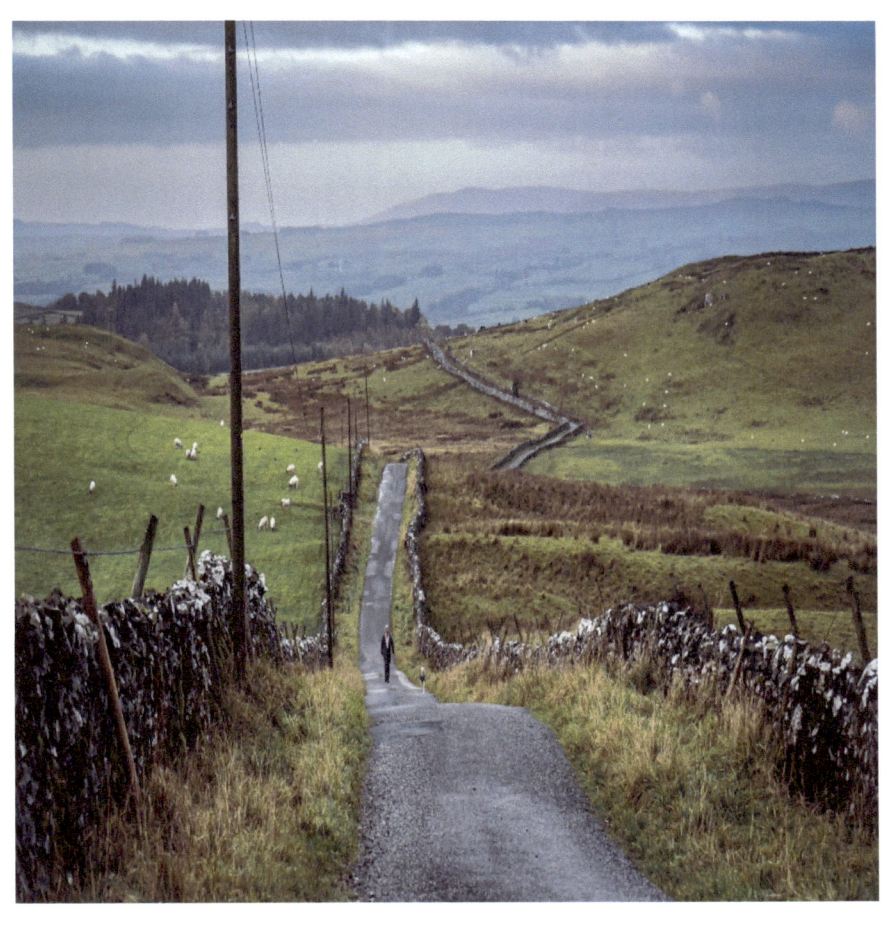

Face on a stone (Castlerigg)

A molar from a bygone beast,
that's lost its way over centuries gone.

Perfectly placed between two dark hills,
like a replacement sycamore.

In a field preventing tractor straight
lines, it's earned the right to exist.

But who is it that hides amongst the
cracks? Who screams, "Let me out!"

Is this Hitchcock, with Alfred lurking,
ready for his cameo?

A brief non-speaking role, but not one
to distract from a giant molar stone.

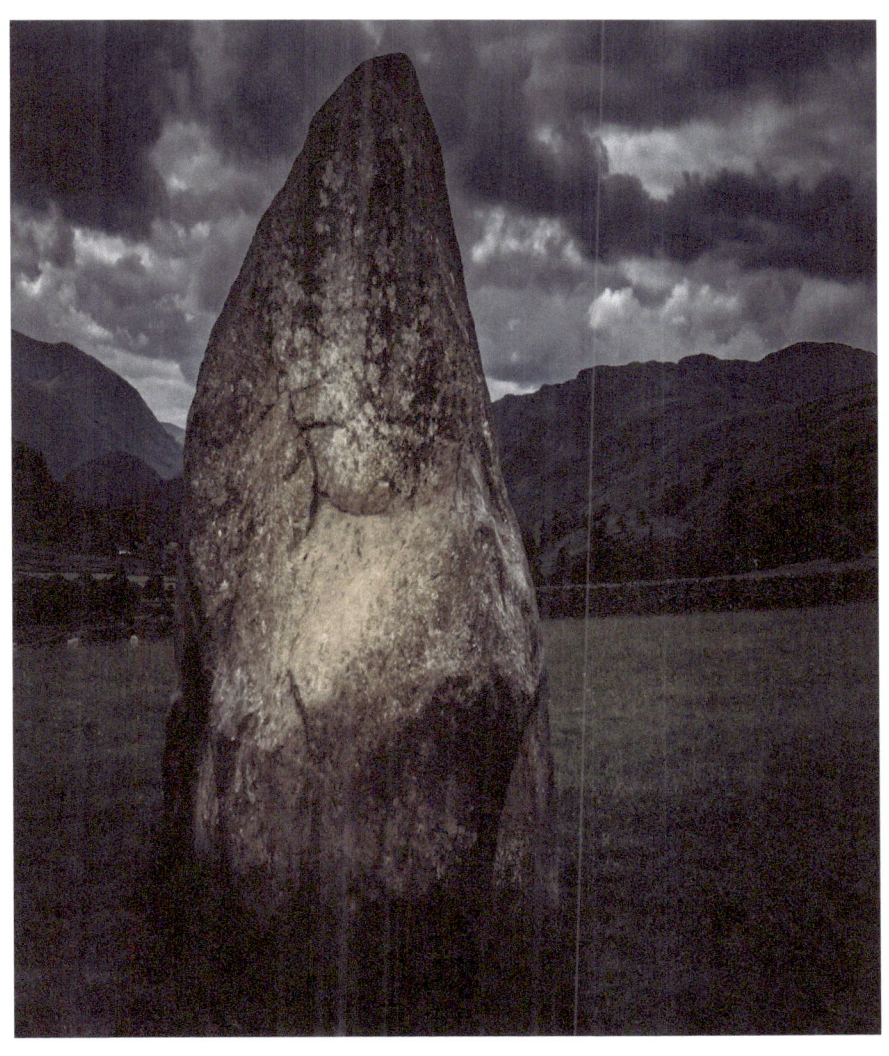

Internet killed the video store

Once a purveyor of Saturday night thrills,
Rom-com heroes, superheroes, horror and crime.

When VHS was king for a while, this store surfed the entertainment wave. Its neon-filled welcoming windows, hinted of joys to be found within.

And for a couple of quid or a fiver, we could lose ourselves in someone else's life.

But technology waits for no one, not even the offer of sweets and cigs could save it.

Now those thrills come, courtesy of the keyboard, and the video store in our home.

The video store lies empty, bright lights hidden by boards. Its painted name fades like its memory.

Soon it won't be remembered at all.

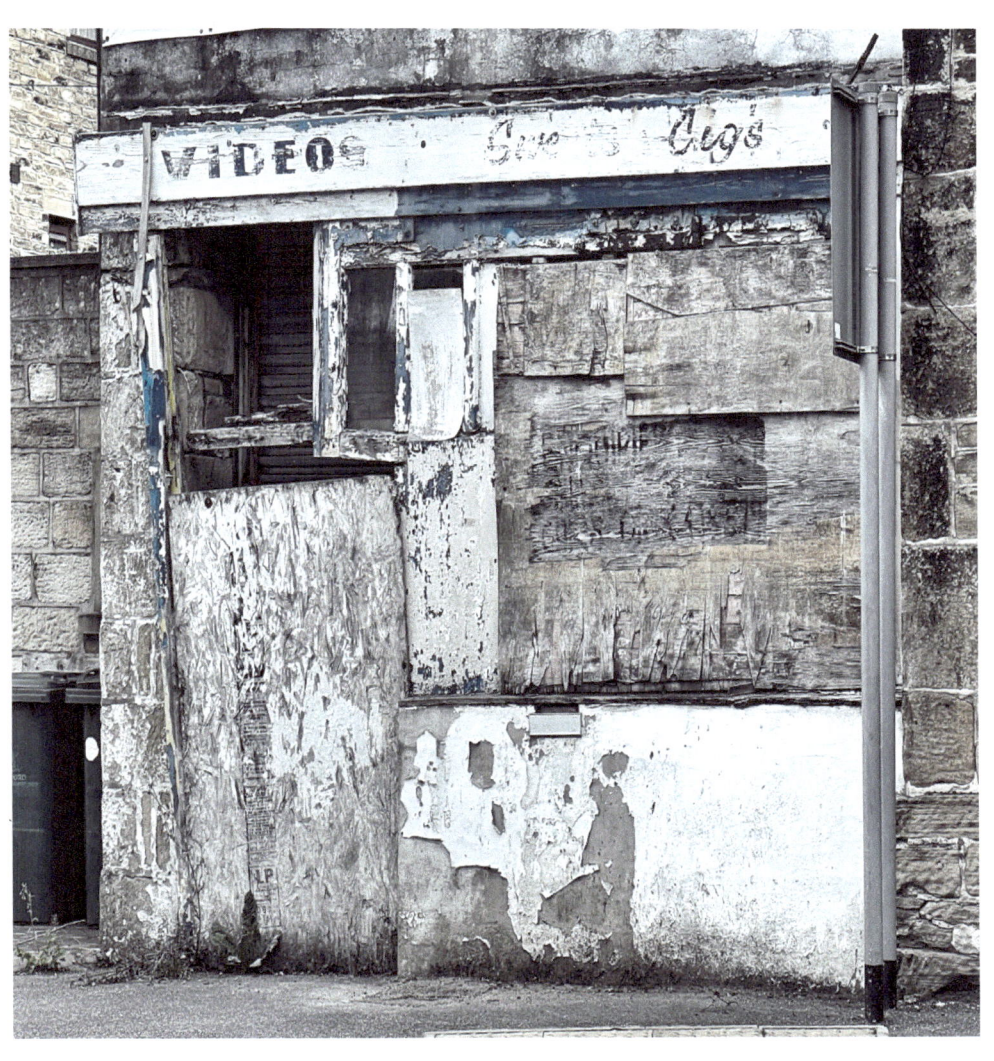

Allium seedhead

Former flower, delicate and fragile, fearing its future in the rain.

An Aztec priest's headdress, birds' feathers of the Quetzalcoatl.

Though beyond its best, it still glistens.

Sacred, its status assured in the rain-soaked garden. It catches the droplets so precious.

It's a green and purple lollipop.

An exploding pyrotechnic of colour, bright and sparkling, a raindrop retainer, in flight.

Supported by just one strong green, tailored stem.

A vertical column, an oiled straw, sucking upwards the nutrients for life.

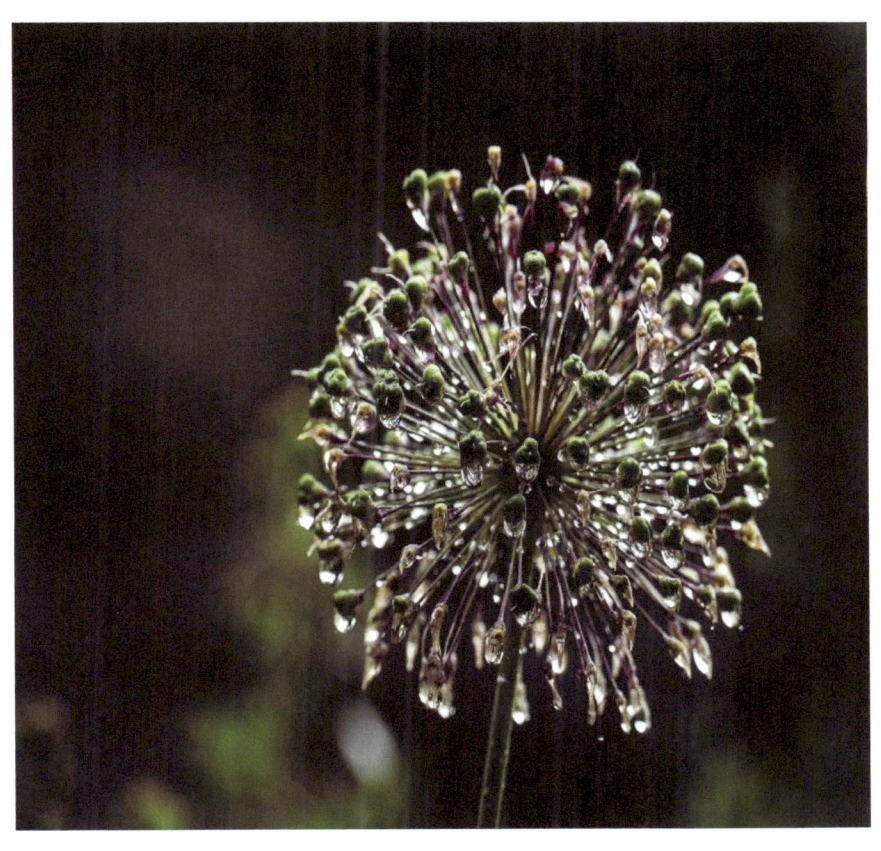

Frozen fence

Man, it was cold!

Wind whipping across the moor,
screaming through the mesh.

Demented choir.

Our only echoes of warmth,
are the woolen tufts, trapped and waving
on shards of metal and glass.

Ice glass.

The sheep are elsewhere today.

Seeking shelter more solid, than this
fierce yet flimsy unforgiving fence.

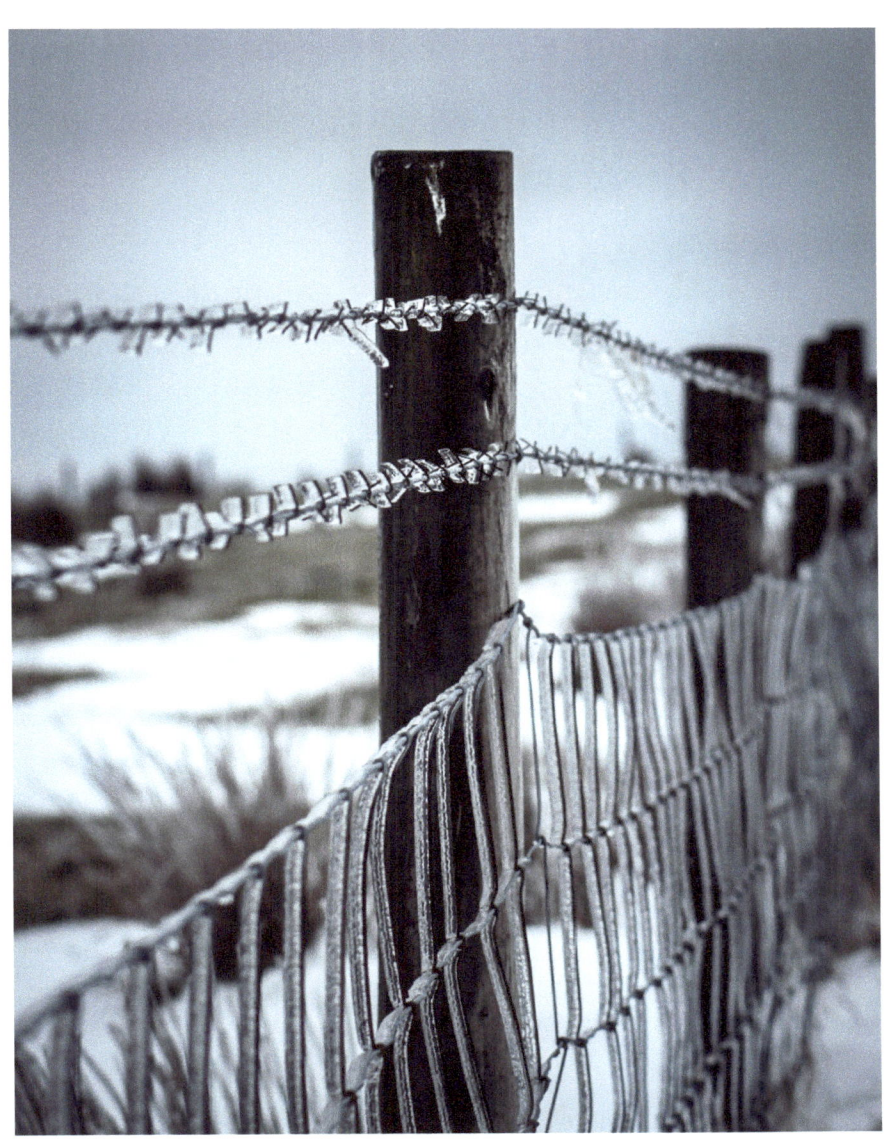

Loneliest bus stop

The route that takes old folk, from
Oxenhope to Hebden Bridge.

No one climbs on here and no one gets off.

Nobody lives nearby. The wind whips
across the sheep filled moors.

A stop for exhausted walkers, those who
want to ride instead and cheat.

The Tour de France in Yorkshire! second
day of the grueling event.

The Brits shout "Froome!", as the peloton
whistles by, navigating the rougher, higher
terrain.

When Heathcliff returned, he alighted the
bus right here.

The Railway Children too, were frequent
flyers.

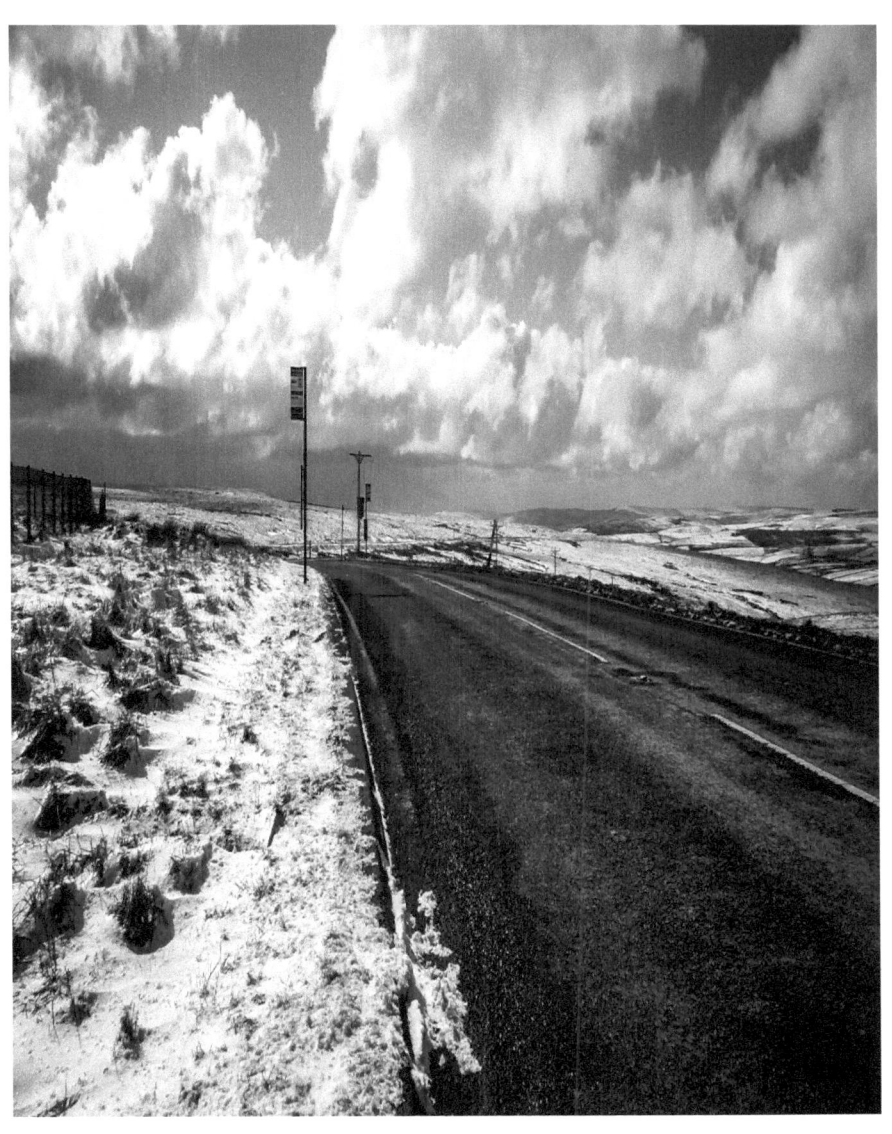

The hidden lake

Like a snowman with a long tail, the
hidden lake exists in denial.

Untouched, no paths or portable toilets or
burger vans in lay-bys.

No fishing rights, nor 'no fishing' signs,
wild doze, untroubled.

No marquees for weddings or jetty
adorned with strange mood lighting.

No way to book a tee time, to view a
monster, to start a conspiracy.

No Airbnb, no photo to be taken, or review
for anyone to be reporting.

A simple tranquil beauty, nestled amongst
the hills and the fir trees.

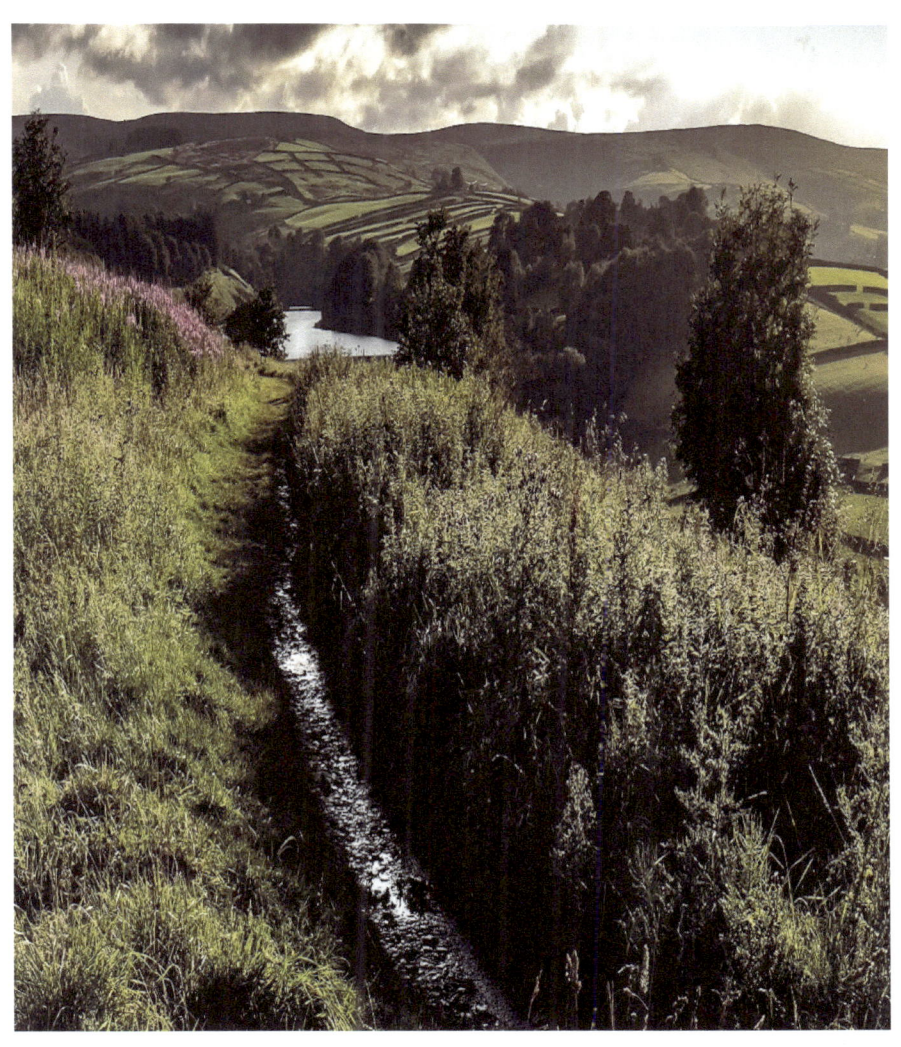

Light in the cloud

Nacreous clouds in the cold and dry,
rainbow clouds with rainbow rings.

Luminescent ice particles, northern
lights, satellites orbiting the earth.

Meteors, ethereal whirlpools of light,
sunlight shining through crystal ice.

Solar storms?

Warped lights from the moon?
UFO's or a military onslaught?

Extraterrestrial life?

Or the whole world waiting forlornly for a
celestial event.

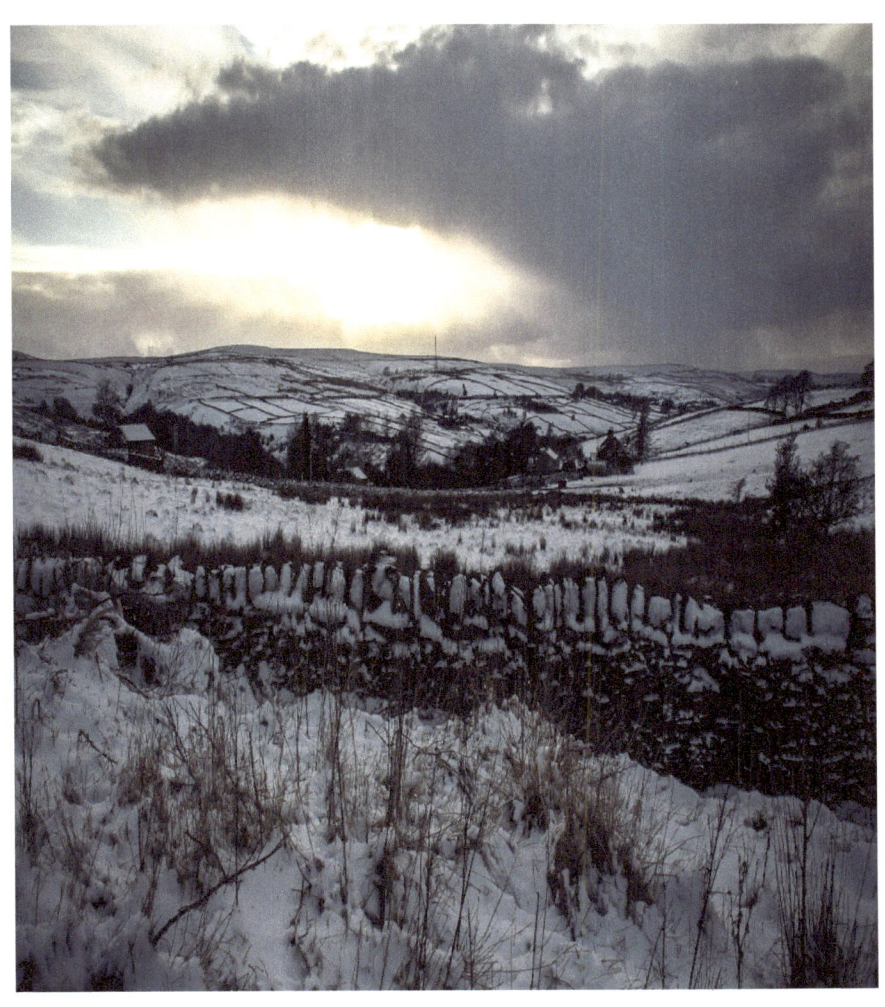

The signpost

A cobbled path that reaches the wall.
A signpost you can't read, when night falls.

Only two ways forward, a limited choice,
tun left or straight on, a calming voice.

Life's T junctions, maybe eight at most,
less choice is more, less to get wrong.

Marriage, divorce, children, your career,
friends to keep and friends to stay clear.

Reach the wall, stand up high, the view
shouts loud, 'you're going the right way'.

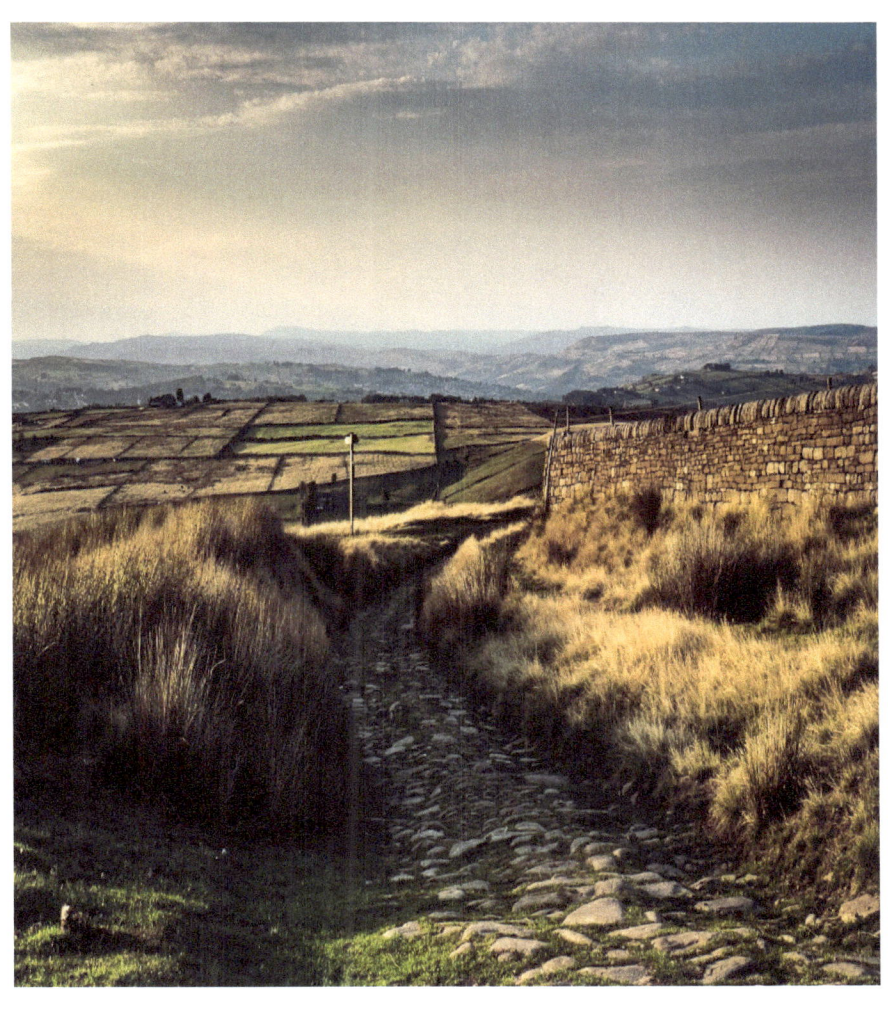

Daybreak

Words hard to find, metaphors unworthy,
cliches common, to describe the scene.

Longfellow celebrates 'the day awakening',
'Stay oh sweet and do not rise' pleads
Donne.

Whilst Oscar rejoices in 'the garden of
Eros', Yeats proclaims, 'no man calls him a
ghost'.

Maya leaves behind 'nights of terror and
fear', for 'daybreak that's wondrously clear
to rise'.

New words are hard to find, romantics own
this scene, in the clear sky above the hills.

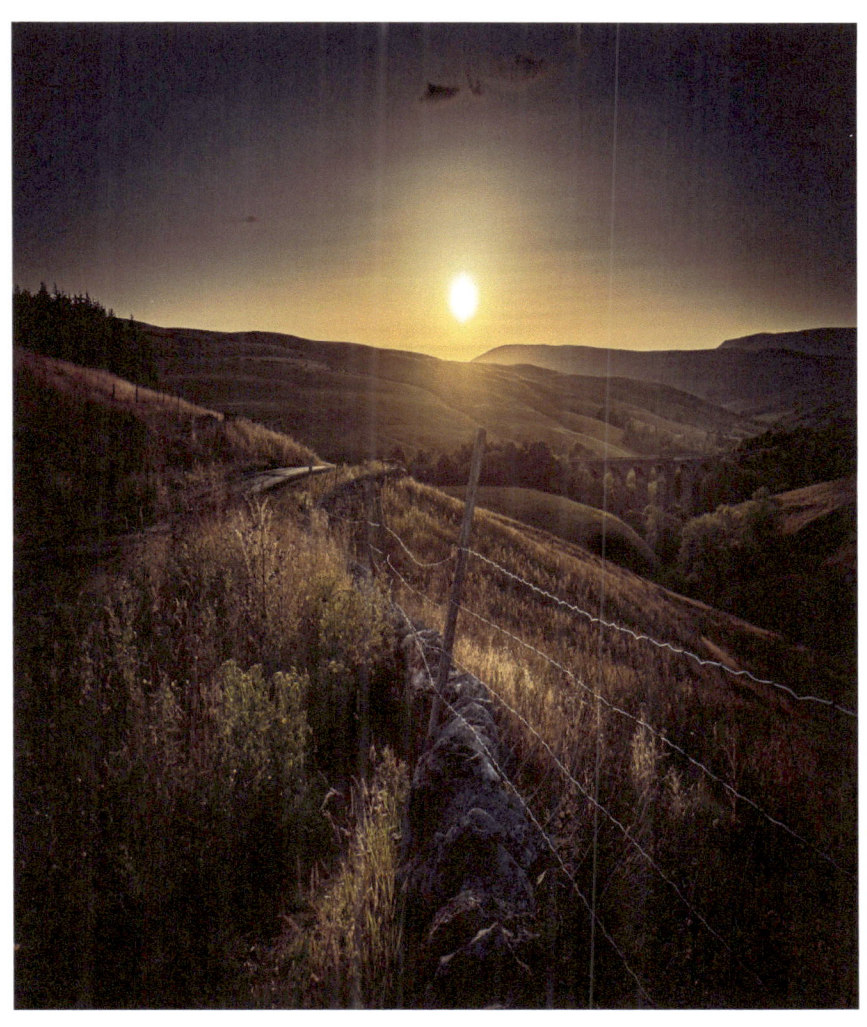

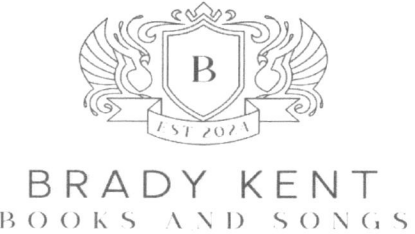

www.ingramcontent.com/pod-product-compliance
Lightning Source LLC
Chambersburg PA
CBHW040259220526
45473CB00002B/532